MARCELLA MARKHAM, who created the idea of *Old is...*,
graduated at the American Academy of Dramatic Art and had a
successful acting career playing many roles on Broadway and
in London's West End. She also appeared in various TV and
film roles. Marcella Markham died in 1991.

DOMINIC POELSMA is famous for the cartoon series
featuring Clive and Augusta every night in the Evening
Standard. He has also illustrated many other books in addition
to *Old is... Great!*

© 1978 Marcella Markham (text)
© 1978 Dominic Poelsma (illustrations)

First published in Great Britain in 1978 by Exley Publications Ltd.
This edition published simultaneously in 1998 by Exley
Publications Ltd in Great Britain, and Exley Publications LLC in
the USA.

ISBN 1-86187-105-8

12 11 10 9 8 7 6 5 4 3 2 1

Edited by Helen Exley.
Written by Marcella Markham.
Illustrated by Dominic Poelsma.
Printed in Hungary.

Exley Publications Ltd, 16 Chalk Hill, Watford, Herts WD1 4BN, UK
Exley Publications LLC, 232 Madison Avenue, Suite 1206, NY 10016, USA.

Old is...
GREAT!

EXLEY
NEW YORK • WATFORD, UK

Old is...

when you prefer a chauffeur driven car to a Ferrari

Old is...

when candlelit tables are no longer romantic
because you can't read the menu

Old is...

when you discover your first grey hair

Old is...

when you go on a political march because you think the exercise will do you good

Old is...

when you wish you had a masseur instead of exercising on the floor

Old is...

when your dentist's bill is astronomical

Old is...

when you think of registering with your doctor
as a hypochondriac

Old is...

when parties don't seem to go with a swing
anymore

when you feel that you don't get out enough
and, would rather stay in, anyway

when you realize nothing is solved after
midnight

when you realize you can't convert anyone to
your point of view and you can't get converted to
anyone else's point of view

when you stop using phrases like "love at
first sight"

when you stop using phrases like "that
indefinable it"

when large parties seem a bore
and dinners for four are madly interesting

when your children tell you that you are
repeating yourself

when you stop using phrases like "animal
magnetism"

when the pension scheme begins to be more
than something you pay into

Old is...

when the men in the office treat you like one of the boys

Old is...

when the young women in the office don't discuss their love lives with you anymore

... and the men do

Old is...

when you wonder if he really means it when
the new office boy says "Hi sexy"

Old is...

when your boss is younger than you are and
a woman

Old is...

Poelsma

when you'd rather skip the office party

Old is...

when a man says "I want to be alone with you"
and you suspect his motives

when a man says "I want to spend the rest of my life with you" and you suspect his sanity!

when you can't fit a lover into your daily routine
... even if yo could find one

when you can't remember what old song reminds you of which old flame

when a cuddle means as much as sex

when you start putting up with men who smoke cigars

when you realise that no matter how many times you walk out you will never leave

when you realise that giving freedom is tying him to you with a great knot

when you demand freedom for yourself

when loyalty means more than love

Old is...

when you regret not having married a millionaire

and you realize one never asked you

Old is...

when you wonder why you have never been
asked to an orgy

Old is...

when you can love a tennis partner just for his game

Old is...

when a banker is more attractive than a film star

Old is...

when you can no longer fall in love without thinking, "What will I do about the children? The furniture?"

Old is...

when you realize there are no pure motives

least of all, your own

Old is...

when Free Love means the freedom to say
"No" firmly

and "Yes" immediately

Old is...

when you can tell the truth openly because no one would believe it anyway

Old is...

when you ask people to guess your age

Old is...

when you tell everyone you're a liberated
woman – and secretly wish someone would
look after you

Old is...

when the telephone wire becomes your
umbilical cord with the world

Old is...

when you don't know if you should wear a
décolleté and show your cleavage

or wear a polo neck to hide the neck lines

Old is...

when you can't remember the original colour of your own hair

Old is...

when you dread the mini skirt might come back into fashion

Old is...

when you stop wanting to be pretty and settle for fascination

Old is...

when styles come back for the second time
and you still have some left from the first time

Old is...

when you just ache to get into something loose

Old is...

when that "rainy day" you have been saving for has arrived

when you wonder if you should have a larger insurance policy
and are certain your husband should

when you give up the fantasy of someone giving you an hour in Harrods to spend all you can

when you make up your mind to live for yourself and, someone in your family needs you right away

when your daughter decides that you and she are different types

when some young boy gives you a seat on public transport

when people automatically start telling you their emotional hang-ups

when candidates for public office are your age or younger

when you buy your own perfume

Old is...

when you stop asking for love

and start giving it

Old is...

when you can't remember the last time you had
sex with your husband

and your husband can't remember either

Old is...

when you admit you don't know everything about sex

Old is...

when you can't be bothered if you have it with the light on or off

Old is...

when your child tells you that you have hair in your nose

Old is...

when your children ask you, "Who was John F. Kennedy and Audrey Hepburn?'

Old is...

when your mother needs <u>your</u> advice

and you're grateful you still have a mother

Old is...

when you start talking to your sister again

Old is...

when your son starts treating you with respect

Old is...

when you're no longer in terror of a head waiter

Old is...

when you admit you actually don't know much about wines

Old is...

when you decide that people will just have to accept you for yourself

Old is...

when you begin to think there are two sides to every story

Old is...

when you look in the mirror and think to yourself
"Aren't I wise?"

Old is...

when you think all your friends are showing their age... but not you

when a metropolitan hotel is more romantic than a country cottage

when you ask an old girl friend, "Tell me honestly, how do I look?"
and you know she won't tell you the truth
and you won't tell her either

when you don't try to hold your tummy in during sex

when you buy something expensive
and don't feel guilty

when you can fart and not blame it on the dog

when a small compliment lifts your ego for more than an hour

when you look better with a few extra pounds on

when you begin thinking "mother knew best"

...GREAT